Copyright Basics
For Artists

By Tom Baxa

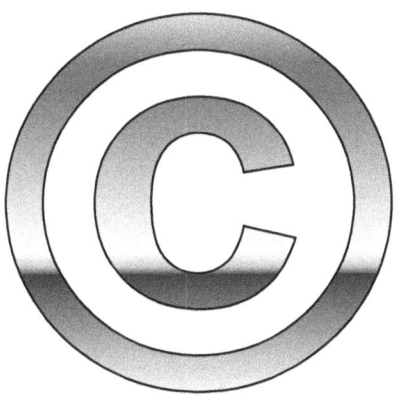

BaxaArt Academy
eBook Series Presentation

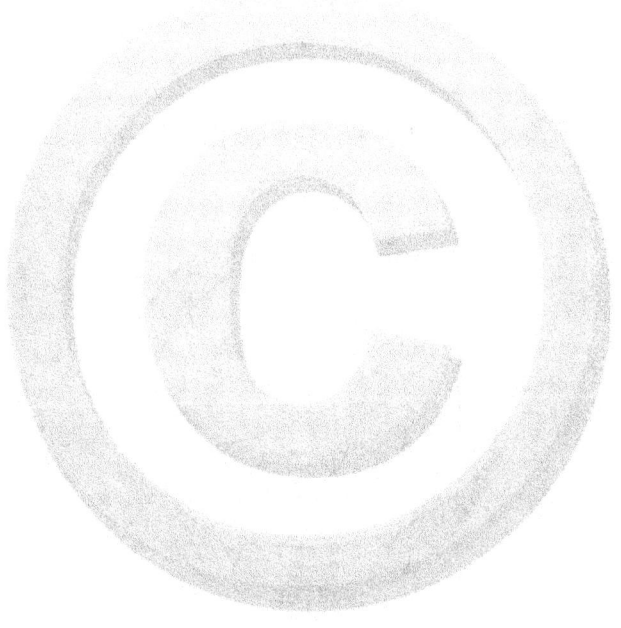

Why You Need This Book

Copyrights are an important part of your life and business as an artist, writer, or other creative. Yet they're seldom taught in school. That's too bad, because **an understanding of copyrights is *critical.***

Unfortunately, the language of copyright law is cryptic, confusing, and very difficult to understand. Luckily, you've found this book! *Copyright Basics for Artists* explains copyrights **in simple terms** and shows you how they apply to you as an artist.

Topics Covered
- What exactly are Copyrights?
- What *do* they protect? What *don't* they protect?
- When are you covered and how long does protection last?
- How to secure and protect your copyrights
- Why it's best to register your work *for full protection under the law*
- Contracts and copyrights
- Confusing and archaic Terms Defined
- The difference between Copyright and Trademark
- And much, much more!

Finally understand Copyrights and how important they are to you as an artist !!

Every time you're presented with a **contract** for an illustration job, the purchase of a painting, a licensing deal, a option for your novel, a full time position as a staff artist, a gallery show, etc., you are being asked to trade your copyrights for a fee. You'd better understand what you're getting into, or you could lose out big time and severely hurt your earning power as a working artist.

READ THIS BOOK and you'll understand Copyrights and how to protect your work!

Published by:

Body Ritual Graphics, Los Angeles, CA

www.BaxaArt.com

www.BaxaArtAcademy.com

First Softcover Edition: August 2014
First eBook Edition: December 2013

10 9 8 7 6 5 4 3 2 1

ISBN 13: 978-0-9905077-1-0

Table of Contents

Disclaimer

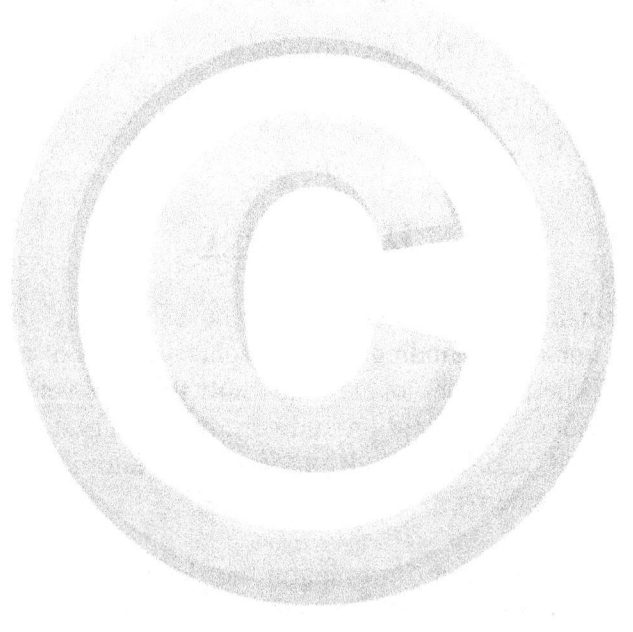

Intro

I'm an artist, just like you. And more than anything, I want to be at the easel painting as much as possible. But there's always a business side to being a working artist, and we have to pay attention to that.

One of the most crucial elements to being a creative person is **the ability to own the exclusive rights to your artwork and being the only one who can profit from it**. This is what copyright law does for you in a nutshell.

Of course, it's the government, so they like to make it much more convoluted than that. And, as you will see, they have their own terminology, some of which is often dated and kind of odd sounding.

www.copyright.gov

The official website of the US Copyright Office is www.copyright.gov, and although it can be pretty confusing at times, **it is the definitive word in copyright law**, along with the language of the actual law of course. (Note: Current copyright law is based on the Copyright Act of 1976 which took effect as of January 1, 1978. There is a lot of confusing language about works created before then and works created after then, etc. You don't have to worry about that because all your works are created after 1978.)

After you get familiar with the basics in this ebook, I recommend that you spend some time at the site and learn more. They have a lot of documentation that you might find helpful. Their circular *Circ40 Registration for Visual Arts* is particularly helpful to start. And you can call or email them with specific questions if you need clarification. You'll also find everything you need to register your work with the US Copyright Office at the site, including filing digitally.

Definition: "Registration" is when you file forms with the US Copyright Office with certain data about your work(s), its author (you), the date it was created, etc. This becomes part of the public record and useful information if you ever have to defend your copyrights in court.

I'm going to try to give you the main things you should know about copyrights, but this ebook is by no means all inclusive. But it will get your head around how things work and why copyrights are important.

Copyrights apply to all things creative like art, music, writing, graphic design, website design, sculpture, spoken word, photography, movies, performances, and more. This ebook is going to focus on how copyrights impact visual artists, but most of the concepts also apply to the other disciplines as well.

As you're reading, some terms may appear that you don't quite understand yet. Keep reading and they will be explained shortly thereafter. I'd also like to mention that I know women are awesome creators as well, but since I am a man writing this ebook, I will often use masculine pronouns to describe people, so please do not take offense.

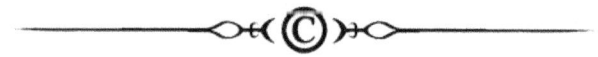

Section 1: Overview

What is a Copyright?

A copyright is a form of protection provided *by the law* to the **"author"** of **"original works of authorship"**, including artistic, literary, dramatic, musical, etc.

> **Definition: "Author" is the term the copyright office uses to describe the person who created a work that can be copyrighted.**

> **Definition: "Original Works of Authorship" refers to the actual work that is created such as a painting, a drawing, a song, a novel, etc. This work must be an original creation by the "author".**

(For the purposes of this ebook I will use the terms "author", "creator", or "artist" to mean the same thing; as well as the terms "work", "piece", "painting" or other types of creative works to mean the same thing as "original works of authorship".)

The owner of a copyright has the exclusive rights to:

- *Reproduce and distribute* the work in copies to the public *for profit*
- Create *derivative works* based upon the work
- *Display (or perform) the work publicly*
- *Authorize others to exploit these rights on his behalf*
- *Transfer all, or a subdivision of, these rights* to another for free or for a fee

Basically copyrights give you, as a creator of a piece of art, the **exclusive** rights to reproduce your work and distribute copies of it for any reason you want, including to making money. You can show it anywhere you want, and create variations on it (derivative works). No one else can use your images unless you give them permission to, either on a handshake or for a price.

Copyrights, especially those registered with the US Copyright Office (USCO), also provide you with legal remedies should someone steal your work (commit copyright **infringement**).

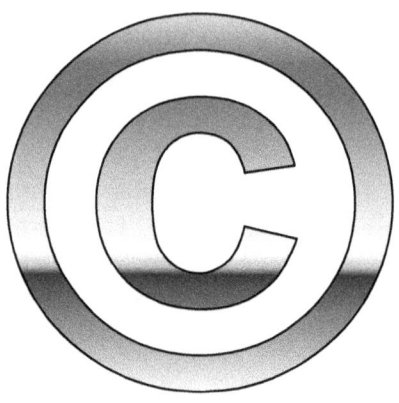

Fixed in a Tangible Medium
In order to be covered by law, a work of art must be **"fixed in a tangible medium"**. Once it is, **you *automatically* own all the copyrights associated with it**. The work does not have to be "finished", published, or even registered with the US Copyright Office, however you gain considerable rights when you do file for registration (See *Section 2: Securing and Protecting Your Rights* below).

> **Definition: "Fixed a tangible medium" is a term that means your idea is documented in a physical, electronic, or digital form that can be readily experienced by anyone. (The copyright office calls these documentations *"copies"*).**

In other words, your cool idea can't just be in your head. You can't sue George Lucas because you had an *idea* for a seven foot tall furry creature called a "mookie". Your idea has to be in a tangible form such as:

- An image painted on canvas or sculpted in clay
- A photograph digitally displayed on a website
- A story printed in on paper
- An audio recording of a poetry reading, etc.

Copyright Notice

A **"copyright notice"** is the notation attached to a work that tells anyone viewing the work, or copies of the work, that it is copyrighted and by whom.

Adding copyright notice to your work with the **copyright date** is done to help protect you in the event that someone uses your work without your permission. Copyright notice and copyright registration with the US Copyright Office is like insurance: it covers you if there is a problem, but if no one ever steals your work, you don't need it and it doesn't really mean anything. But since your images are your greatest asset as an artist, it's best to protect yourself.

A copyright notice should appear in the form "**Copyright or ©, year first published, copyright owner's name**". If the work is unpublished, use the **year of completion** as the copyright date.

In addition to the notice above, some foreign countries require the phrase **"All Rights Reserved"** also be included at the end of the copyright notice, so you may want to include it whenever space allows.

Works do not have to be registered for you to attach a copyright notice, and you don't have to have notice attached to insure your copyrights (although you used to have to attach notice prior to 1976). But it is best to get in the habit of doing it regardless, because it helps provide *proof* of ownership and date of publication if there is an infringement.

See *Section 2: Securing and Protecting Your Rights: Copyright Notice: Copyright Date for Your Copyright Notice* below for more information about copyright notices and dates.

Publication
"Publication" is defined by copyright law as the **distribution of copies of a work to the public** in a tangible form like in print, audio recording, video disc, via digital delivery, or by other means.

Simply displaying original art at a convention *is not* considered publication, however your art in a flyer that is distributed to the public at the con, *is* considered publication.

Unfortunately, the law still has not caught up with technology. As is stands at the time of this writing, **it is not definitive as to whether or not showing your art on a website is considered publication**. In other words, there has not been sufficient case law on the matter for the copyright office to say with certainty one way or the other as a point of law.

Here's where it gets a little tricky. If the image you are showing on your website is **designed to be downloaded and shared**, for free or for profit (like a downloadable print, a book to be printed out, a wallpaper, a screen saver), or generally designed for mass distribution other than just for casual viewing, then it is considered publication. If you post images to sites like Café Press where consumers can create products with your works on them, then those images are definitely considered published.

It is very odd to me that ebooks, pdfs, video files, or even jpegs are not definitively considered "copies" of a work and that sharing digital files is not considered "distribution of copies", but that's where the law stands for now.

As is always the case, the law will eventually catch up with technology, so **I would err on the side of caution and the minute you post something on the web consider that it is published** and that you have 90 days from that day to register it with the copyright office to receive full protection under the law (more on this later).

What is Covered by Copyrights?

The following is a list of categories of copyrightable works. The categories are broad and cover a wide range of works. So the artwork category would include things like: paintings, drawings, sketches, handmade books, graphic design, website design, jewelry design, fabric graphics, photography, sculpture, ceramics and all kinds of other "visual arts". Oddly, typefaces and calligraphy are not copyrightable unless they make the letters into a piece of art. Here are the categories:

1. Pictorial, graphic, and sculptural works [ARTWORK]
2. Motion pictures and other audiovisual works
3. Literary works
4. Musical works, including any accompanying words
5. Sound recordings
6. Dramatic works, including any accompanying music
7. Pantomimes and choreographic works
8. Architectural works

Derivative works

A "**derivative work**" is a new work created by an author that is *based on or integrates material from an already existing work* previously created by the same author.

A derivative work must be original and created solely by you. You can't incorporate *another* artist's work, change it around, add some stuff, and call it yours. It has to be based on *your own* original work.

Derivative works, if significantly different than the original, can be copyrighted as a new work. Making minor changes or additions of little substance to a preexisting work will not qualify the work as a new version for copyright purposes.

Examples of Derivative Works
- A painting of a character you created in an earlier painting
- Sculpture (based on your drawing)
- A series of works based on a similar visual motif
- A collage or photo montage that incorporates imagery from an earlier work
- Drawing (based on your photograph)
- Motion picture (based on a play)
- Novel in English (a translation of a book published in Russian)
- Sound recording (where two of the 10 songs were previously published or remixed)
- Musical arrangement (based on a public domain work by Bach)

Copies and Reprints

"**Copies**" of a work are some form of tangible item that can be distributed like an art print, t-shirts or other products with your image on them, cds, dvds, books, etc., usually with the intent of publication and distribution. Digital files can also be considered copies. Something is a copy if the original work is essentially unaltered and just reproduced in another form.

A "**reprint**" is a different form or version of the *same* content. For example: a softcover or an eBook is a reprint of the hardcover version of a novel. Reprints do not require separate copyright registration. An audio book, however, is considered a performance and thus a derivative work and requires a separate copyright.

What is NOT Covered by Copyrights?

Here are some of the major categories of things that are not covered by copyrights:

- Works that have not yet been fixed in a tangible form (like a dance that hasn't been filmed, or an impromptu speech that wasn't written down or recorded)
- Works consisting entirely of common information with no original content (like a calendar, a list taken from public records, etc.)
- Titles, company or brand names, slogans or catch phrases like Tom Baxa "Creepazoid Artist" [these fall under trademark coverage]
- Text logos or images that represent a brand (like the Macintosh Apple logo) [trademark]
- Procedures, methods, systems, concepts, devices, inventions (stuff like a system you have for mixing paint, or the procedures for emulating the structure of a Japanese company, your idea for an invention). [these items fall under Patent coverage] However you may copyright a written explanation of an idea, or an illustration of your new invention.

How Long Does Protection Last?

Copyright protection begins when a work is fixed in tangible form and extends for **the life of author + 70 years**. If two or more artists worked on the same piece (a joint work), then copyright lasts 50 years beyond death of the last surviving contributor. Works for hire extend 95 years from publication or 120 years from creation, whichever is shorter.

Once the copyright on a work expires, the work is considered to be in the **public domain**, which means that the work is no longer protected by any copyrights and can be used freely by anyone for any reason, including for profit.

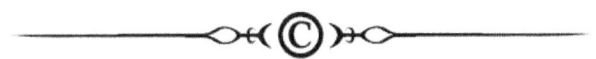

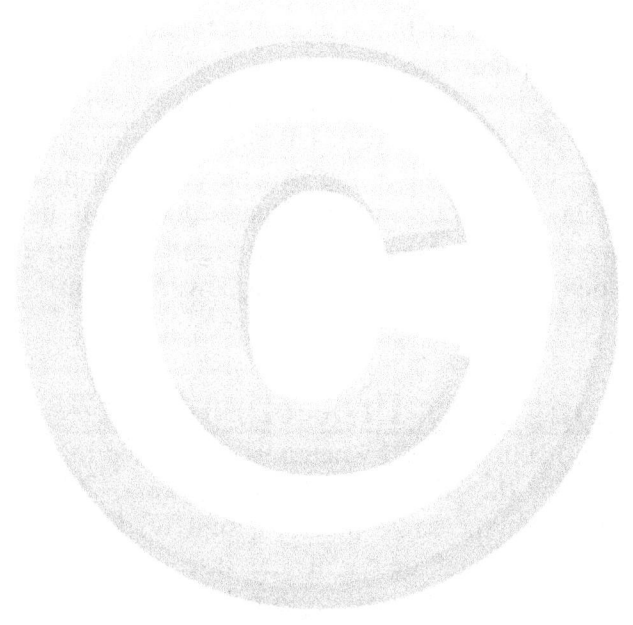

Section 2:Securing and Protecting Your Rights

It's important to understand copyrights and to do your part to protect your rights. Right now you may be just starting out and thinking that it's not that important, but I'm sure you plan on growing your career, so artwork that you make today may be very valuable to you in the future. That's why you want to protect it now.

> **Definition: "Copyright Infringement" is when someone violates your copyright protection, usually in the form of using your work, in whole or in part, without your permission.**

Copyright Notice

Even though your work is copyrighted the minute it is fixed in a tangible medium, and an unpublished work is at very little risk of being stolen or plagiarized since few people are seeing it, it is still a good idea to attach copyright notice to your work and any copies of it.

A copyright notice is your first line of defense, and it tells everyone viewing your work that it is protected and that you understand what that means.

What should you put a copyright notice on? EVERYTHING. Your paintings, prints, social media postings, jpegs, blog postings, website postings, images in a book, images reproduced in your portfolio, merchandise you create with the image, etc. Why not, it's free.

Always put a copyright notice on *your own work* to help identify you as the creator and owner of the copyright. It's best to have the copyright notice on the actually image, instead of just in the text below it on a page, especially with digital copies. That way if someone borrows or shares the image, the copyright is already attached. I like to paint the © symbol with my signature on a painting that I own the rights to.

Some work for hire contracts may grant you the limited right you to show the work you created, like in your portfolio or on your website, even though you may not own the copyright. In this case, you are usually required to attach notice, with the company as the copyright owner, to any images you show in print, digitally, or otherwise.

Obviously, with a digital image file like a jpeg, your signature and copyright notice can be cropped or painted out. So you may consider editing the meta data on an image file. A lot of casual infringers aren't aware of this feature that is embedded in image files. Do so by opening the image in Photoshop, then going to File > File Info. This will bring up a dialog box with all kinds of meta data fields that you can fill. You can include your name, image title, description, urls, keywords for search engines, and a copyright notice.

You can also embed a **digital watermark** into an image file in addition to putting the copyright notice on the image. A digital watermark is a mark or writing that is imperceptibly put into an image on a pixel level by a software program. You need the program or a graphics program that supports it to see the watermark. Adobe has a great help file on this topic and they support Digimarc (www.digimarc.com). You don't really have to go to this extent, but the option is available to you.

<u>Copyright Date for Your Copyright Notice</u>
A copyright notice contains the name of the copyright owner and a date, that not only tells others that the work is protected, but can also help prove when a work was created in the event that you find yourself having to prove it in a court of law.

However, it is often difficult to *prove* when a work is *created*, even if you keep good records or attach notice, so it's not a bad idea to register the work shortly after you complete it. That way you have documented and dated proof as to when the work was created (or very close to it). Publishing is another excellent way to attach a provable date to a work. It's important to *register* the work when you publish to avail yourself of the full protection of the law.

The Copyright Office says that a copyright notice should appear in the form "**Copyright or ©, year first published, copyright owner's name**". This is accurate, although this is a bit misleading in its absoluteness. Let me clarify things a bit.

If your work is unpublished, the date you should use in your copyright notice is the **"year of completion"**, or the year that you finished the work.

The **first date of publication** is used as the copyright notice date when it applies to an item or product that is published like a book, a cd, a movie, etc., or a published form of the work like a print of a painting.

The **individual works that go in or on that published item continue to use their year of completion as the copyright notice date**, but the published collected work that they are a part of (like a book, a portfolio, a compilation cd, etc.) uses the publication date. For Example: *Dragon painting #1* © 1986, *Dragon painting #2* © 1994, and *Zombie painting* © 1991 make up the published *BaxaArt Portfolio* © 2013.

So even though your published portfolio is copyrighted © 2013 Thomas M. Baxa, the individual works within **each have their own copyright date based on their year of completion**, and you continue to use the year of completion for those individual works. You *don't* change their copyright notice dates to the publication date once they are published.

Individual Works:
Copyright Date = Year of Completion
Published Item:
Copyright Date = Year First Published

Here's why this distinction is important. Let's say you do a painting in 1990. You attach notice to it in the form © 1990 Thomas M. Baxa, with the year of completion as the date. If you publish in 1990, then using the publication date as the copyright notice date would be just fine.

But what if you don't publish the work until 2010? That's a 20 year difference between the completion date and the publication date. Should that work be infringed, you want all your notices to reflect the date it was completed.

Now, if the work has changed in a significant way from the day you completed it to the day you published it, then the altered version would be considered a derivative work and you would use the first date of publication on your copyright notice for the "new" derivative work.

Date Range
What if a work took more than one year to create? Even though you've probably see copyright notices with a date range like © 2011-2012, technically you are only supposed to list **one** year, the year the work was completed or published, not a range.

Effective Date of Registration
When you register your work with the US Copyright Office, you are issued an **"Effective Date of Registration"** (also called the registration date). This is the official *registration* date for the work, but you never put the Effective Date of Registration as your copyright notice date.

The value of the registration date is that it can act as proof in a court of law as to when the work was registered and whether or not it was published; because when you file for registration you must provide copies of the work, and if the work is published you provide copies of the work in published form.

The registration date cannot prove *when a work is actually created*, but it can help, especially if you register soon after the work is created. If you wait until the work is published to register, even if it is years after creation, then the publication date is your best chance at *proving* the creation date, but you may have lost some protection during the gap in years between creation and publication.
In any case, you should keep your own records of when a work is first completed in case you have to defend your copyright. But one good thing is that you can register a work when completed and still unpublished, and don't have to re-reregister when published. To get *full protection* under the law you must register a work 90 days after publication. Keep reading to understand the requirements for full protection under the law.

Should I Register My Work with the US Copyright Office?

What is the US Copyright Office?
The US Copyright Office (or USCO), a part of the Library of Congress, is the official government body, that collects and maintains all the records of copyright registration. Its database is used as proof of copyright ownership in the United States.

Registered copyrights are considered *public records* so anyone can request copies and view them at the US Copyright Office and their website. So only provide the information they require.

Once you register a work with the USCO, you are issued a **Certificate of Registration** with and **Effective Date of Registration** as proof of the official registration. (See below)

Keep Your Own Records

Keeping track of your most valuable assets, your artwork, is critically important whether you register them with the copyright office or not.

Include the date of completion *on your actual work* so you know what year it was created, and keep an organized database of some kind to keep track of your work.

When you register your work with the Copyright office, it's basically being logged into an antiquated filing system that houses millions of works, so it's a good practice to keep your own records as well.

Here's a good example: When you register a collection, let's say a grouping of 20 paintings, the USCO logs it as one record and can only search for that one record – the collection. A search cannot find *Painting #14: Blue Sky* within the collection. So you are responsible for remembering what works are held within a collection you register.

Since you can file a pdf as documentation for your work, I keep a copy of the pdf and the filed form in my records so I can search it myself. Then if I need a copy of the official record from the

USCO, then I can request the record for *Collection: 20 Paintings* and I know that *Painting #14: Blue Sky* is in there.

I also keep a log of the copyrights I've filed, the dates filed and accepted, and all the important details about the registration. Here's an actual entry from my log:

Sample Copyright Log		
Date	**Work**	**Filing Type**
9/8/10	Title: **Blood Rituals: The Art of Tom Baxa**	Printed copy $35
Actual pdf file name: na – Sent 2 physical books		
Check cashed on: 09/09/10		
Certificate arrived: 11/10/10		
Effective Date of Registration: 09/30/10 **Registration #: VA 1-XXX-X**		
Case # 746XXX filed electronically 9/8/10, pd $35 electronically confirm#562XX		

There's an old trick of sealing up a copy of your work and mailing it to yourself, and keeping it sealed in your files once you receive it. Mailing yourself a copy of your work *does not give you any added copyright protection.* What it DOES do is help **prove the date that the work was created** because it is sealed in an envelope with the date in the post mark stamped on it. This can be useful if going to court is necessary and can be an inexpensive part of your record keeping regiment.

Why it's Best to Register Your Work

It is ideal to register your work with the copyright office whenever possible because it **gives you the most protection under the law**. However, as you and I know, we create hundreds of images every year and it's not feasible financially to pay $35 a pop to register every work. Luckily, the law provides some provisions to register after an infringement occurs, but you aren't as well protected by the law.

As a rule, you can wait to register your work until it's published, or made public like on your website. Until then there's no way anyone can steal it, because you're the only one who knows it exists. If you intend on posting a work on the web or publishing it, that's when it's exposed to other people and you may choose to protect it.

The law states that a registered unpublished work does not have to be registered again once it is published.

Some Reasons You Might Want to Register a Work:
- It's going be featured prominently in your marketing efforts in print or on the web
- It's going to be widely distributed on a product by you or a company
- It contains characters that are pivotal to your intellectual property
- You've been infringed before and are leery of repeat offenses
- You're planning on adding it to a product in the near future
- There is a lot of fan interest in your work and it is quickly spread over the web once made public
- And more.

Register Drafts and Early Versions
On works that may take a long time to finish or projects that are critically important to you like the development of a new intellectual property, it's not a bad idea to copyright rough drafts, sketches, or early versions of works you intend to finish, because it protects the work from its earliest inception.

Remember, you can register an unpublished work, and don't have to re-reregister when published. And if new drafts are significantly different than earlier versions, you should register them separately as derivative works.

Importance of Publication

- If a work is published, you have added proof should it be infringed
- Works that are published in the US get deposited in the Library of Congress.
- The year of publication may determine the duration of copyright protection for anonymous works and works for hire.
- When a work is published, it identifies the year of publication, the name of the copyright owner, and informs the public that the work is protected by copyright.

Full protection under the law

You are granted copyright ownership the minute you create something in a tangible form. However, you lose considerable protection and legal remedy power if you don't **register the work** with the copyright office.

For maximum protection: Reregister your work with the USCO *before* someone infringes, or within 90 days after publication. If your work is infringed upon, you can still file afterwards for up to 5 years after publication, but you will have limited protection. Registration is *required* in order to file a lawsuit, so if you wait longer than 5 years after publication, you may not be able to bring suit.

The number one reason to register your work is that it makes it economically feasible to defend your copyrights in court if your work has been infringed.

If you didn't register a work, it's extremely likely you won't be able to afford to hire an attorney to help you stop an infringement because the costs of mounting a lawsuit are not reimbursed even if you win the suit.

If you have registered a work before infringement, a **lawyer will be more likely to take your case and work on a contingency basis** (which means they get paid only when the lawsuit is won) because it's easier to prove your case, their fees will be covered if you win, and more damages can be awarded.

What is Covered if You Do Register

If you do find yourself in court after all other attempts to remedy the situation fail, having a registered copyright will provide the following protections and advantages that support your case and help you recoup lost monies and court costs if you win:

- **Registration is required in order to even file a lawsuit** for a violation of copyright
- A Certificate of Registration filed before infringement is considered *"prime-facie* evidence", which means the court considers it **probable proof** that the copyright is in fact valid, that the statements within the copyright application are truthful, and that the work was created before the infringement.
- A Certificate of Registration **fixes the date for the creation of the work**
- Registration helps prevent an infringer from claiming certain ignorances
- Court ordered **Injunctive Relief**
- **100% Reimbursement of all court fees** including but not limited to: attorney, court, filing, deposition, expert fees
- Recovery of **Actual Damages** suffered from an unauthorized use of a work, including any profits the infringer made on your work
- Recovery of **Statutory Damages.** If actual damages can't be established, the law provides for statutory damages, or set amounts of money awarded to the copyright holder.
- Recovery of **Additional Damages** in certain circumstances

Definition: "Injunctive Relief" or the act of "Enjoining" is when the court orders the infringer to remedy and refrain from doing certain acts, like using your artwork. This might mean removing your work from his website, recalling a print run that has your image in it, etc.

Definition: "Actual Damages" is the amount of money that you could have made on your work had it not been infringed, and often includes any profits the infringer made on your work. Actual damages can be measured, like the loss of wages, and have to be proven, which can often be difficult when copyright infringement is concerned.

Definition: "Statutory Damages" are predetermined payments established in the language of the law to compensate for certain injuries, in this case, infringement of your copyrights. Statutory damages are sometimes made available because it is too difficult to calculate Actual Damages or as punitive measures against the defendant.

Statutory Damages range from $750 - $30,000 per work infringed. If you can prove that the infringement was willful and intentional you may be entitled to statutory damages up to $150,000 per work. However, infringers who can show that they were "not aware and had no reason to believe" they were infringing on a copyright may have the damages reduced to $200 per work.

Ultimately, the final judgment in any copyright case lies with the judge. He may decide that you win the case, but award you very little damages, or he may enjoin the infringement and not award you any monetary compensation. Every case is different, as is every outcome.

Importance of Copyright Registration	
Registered before Infringement	**Unregistered or Registered After Infringement**
100 % Fees and Costs Paid (Lawyer Fees, court, filing, deposition, expert costs)	No Fees paid
Injunctive Relief	Injunctive Relief
Actual Damages can be awarded	Only **Actual Damages** paid (you have to prove the amount of lost profits)
Statutory Damages ($750-30k per work) You don't have to prove actual profits lost, the court determines this If infringement is willful, the court may award up to $150k per work infringed regardless of how much money they made on your work	No Statutory Damages awarded
Additional Damages can be awarded	No Additional Damages

How to Register Your Work with the US Copyright Office

I'm not going to go into great detail about the registration process. You can find all the instructions you need to file at the copyright site. But I will lay out the broad strokes.

You can mail in your filing, or do it electronically at the copyright office site. Electronic filings are cheaper and easier, you can upload digital copies as your deposit, have a faster processing time, track the application status, and pay with a credit card. The entire process takes about 2-5 months from start to finish.

Make sure all three of the requirements below are included in the envelope or efiling. Circulars *Circ 40 Registration for Visual Arts* and *Circ 40a Deposit Requirements for Registration Claims to Copyright in Visual Arts Material* will get you started. Review the requirements carefully at the USCO site because if you omit something or make a mistake, the application may get delayed or rejected.

Filing Requirements

1. Fill out **form VA** for visual art works accurately and completely
2. Pay a non-refundable **fee of $35 per filing** to register online, $65 for mailed registration
3. **"Deposit" 2 complete copies** of your work in an acceptable form for the record. (This can be a physical copy of the published work like a book, a photo of a sculpture, a printout of a large painting, a cd or dvd with a collection, a pdf, etc.)

While your application is being reviewed you will be able to track its progress, and will eventually be issued an official physical paper **"Certificate of Registration"**, which you should file and safeguard like any important document (like your birth certificate). This is the documented proof of the copyright protection for your work and you may need it sometime in the future.

Even though it may take a little while for the USCO to issue the actual certificate, the **"Effective Date of Registration"** is the date that the copyright office receives your accurately filed form, your deposit or copy of your work, and the fee. The Registration Date is the official date that gets attached to your work and is used as proof in a court of law.

If you need to make a change to one of your records, the USCO has forms for that. It's also very important that you keep your address current if you move.

You register a derivative work with the VA form just as if it were an original work. And if there are "joint authors", or two or more contributors to a work, you should list all of them on the VA form.

Registering Multiple Unpublished Works as a Collection

You can register a **"Collection"** or group of **unpublished** works (they don't even have to be related) and give the collection a title like *25 Monsters from 2013*. It's a good way to get a bunch of images registered for a lot less money, and there is no limit to the amount of works you can include.

But the titles of the individual works in the group are not noted in the record, so you can't search for them. You have to remember what monster drawings were in that record if you ever have to prove it; the copyright office cannot search into groups. So keep good records.

Since the law states that a registered unpublished work does not have to be registered again once it is published, a good strategy, especially if you are self publishing over time, would be to register a bunch of unpublished works as one collection and pay one fee, then you don't have to reregister them again once they are eventually published.

Publish, and Register a Bunch of Works at Once

If you register a compilation item like an art book, *every image in the book is considered registered under the single registration* for the book. In one fell swoop you can register a bunch of your art for one fee.

International Copyright Protection

This is a complicated issue, so I won't be covering it here, but suffice it to say **that there is no such thing as international copyright protection** that covers every country. Each country has their own laws governing copyrights and how they treat other countries' copyright laws.

The two main international copyright conventions are the *Berne Convention* (the US adhered to the *Berne Convention* on March 1st 1989) and the *Universal Copyright Convention.* If you're going to be doing a lot of business in other countries with your copyrighted works or intellectual properties, I suggest you meet with a copyright attorney and determine your coverage.

United States Only

Unfortunately, iron clad copyright protection extends to the United States ONLY unless you apply for international copyrights. So if you see your art on a t-shirt in China, there's not a lot you can do about it without spending a ton of money on lawyers, since you don't technically own the copyright for that region. However, most countries do offer protection to foreign works under certain conditions spelled out in international copyright treaties and conventions.

Note About Creative Commons Licenses

You may have seen Creative Commons copyright licenses on some of your favorite sites alongside user created or uploaded content.

Creative Commons.org is a non-profit organization, in no way associated with the US Copyright Office, which has offered a free legal tool and a system for creatives to *license* their copyrighted work to users on the web and elsewhere. Their system essentially grants various levels of permission to use a copyrighted work that is easy to understand and widely accepted.

However, Creative Commons licenses are not an alternative to copyrights. It's more like a pre-determined contract between you, the copyright owner, and the end user who wants to use your image much like the Terms Of Use statements on websites, that basically say that if you use this site, you agree to these terms.

The enforceability against an infringement based on Creative Commons licenses is not ironclad, and any rights you grant under them should, in my opinion, be done so sparingly and with caution. You can read more about it at http://creativecommons.org.

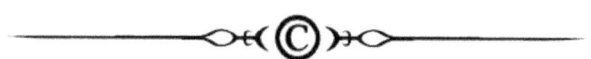

Section 3: Contracts and Other Legal Matters

Copyrights are a matter of federal and state law, so it is always advisable to get expert legal advice where they are concerned. But that can be expensive. In many cases, you can get along by educating yourself out of books, etc. in order to know your rights, recognize infringements, and understand contracts. But if you're brokering a big deal or your livelihood is being threatened by a hardcore court case, you want a lawyer that is on your side.

Do I need a Lawyer?

There are attorneys that specialize in intellectual property, copyright and trademark law. As I said before, copyright law can be tricky and hard to understand, and it's open to interpretation. If you want it done right and you can afford a copyright attorney, then by all means you should hire one.

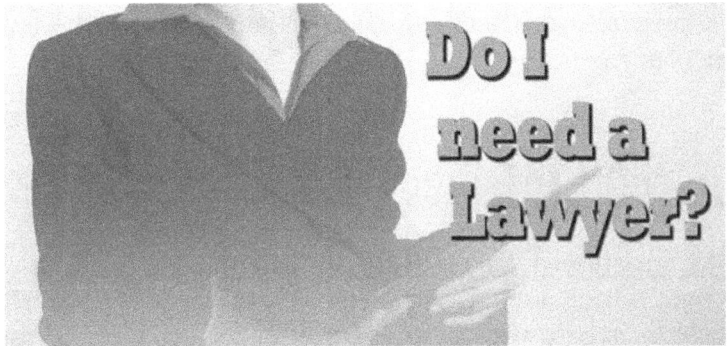

There are some great advantages to hiring an attorney:
- They know the law inside and out, without any misunderstanding
- They have experience from years of practice and other cases similar to yours

- They are *on your side* and are reviewing/drafting contracts with *your best interest in mind*
- Any company you enter an agreement with is going to try to slant things to their advantage – every time. You need to know what to look for
- They will file the necessary papers in a timely fashion to secure your rights

As an illustrator for hire, things are often pretty cut and dry. If you're doing a deal with a large and reputable company, they have staff lawyers that have drafted a contract in accordance with the law. Of course, they've slanted the contract in their favor – that's what companies do.

If you have a basic understanding of copyrights and contract clauses regarding them, you can usually review a contract yourself to, if nothing else than to check for red flags that you should investigate further.

If you have an intellectual property that you've created and want to protect it, grow it, and profit from it, you may find it necessary to hire a lawyer so that you can take full advantage of the law and secure your rights.

Copyright Infringement

What Constitutes Copyright Infringement
Copyright infringement is when someone either uses your artwork, in whole or in part, without your permission (unauthorized use); or copies elements of your artwork in a work that they create.

It is a myth that it is ok to use 10% of someone else's work in your own. You may likely get away with it, but if someone comes after you, it is always up to a judge to decide if there was an infringement.

The legal test of infringement is that the infringing work has a **"substantial similarity"** to the original, which roughly translates into whether an ordinary observer would recognize a work as copied in whole or in part from an earlier one.

Unauthorized Use

Many laypeople do not understand copyrights and have no idea that works in a magazine or especially on the web are not free for them to use as they please. It's easy to see their confusion, especially with the way images are shared in today's Web 2.0 environment and on social media sites. Therefore it is not uncommon for people to use your image to jazz up their websites or as their avatar on social media.

Technically this is an unauthorized use of your copyrighted work. But you have to decide what is acceptable to you and what is not, and what is worth taking action against and what is not.

Fans love to create art gallery sites that showcase their favorite artists. While this is flattering, if they didn't ask your permission, it's a copyright infringement. But you can also look at it as free advertising and beneficial to your career. If they are using your art to generate traffic to their site so they can sell their products or charge for advertising, this might not sit well with you. Again, you have to weigh what's acceptable to you because you can't fight every battle – you've got art to make!

Unfortunately, some people just don't have any scruples and will steal your work and try to make a profit off of it, figuring they won't get caught, or that you won't have the stones or the financial resources to stop them. There are times when you feel you have to take action. I've outlined some courses of action below in the section called *What to do if Your Copyrights are Infringed.*

There have been a rash of digital artists stealing artwork off the web and panning it off as their own in online portfolios in order to get jobs. This is an egregious assault and you should deal with that immediately.

The "Fair Use" Exception

Section 107 of the copyright law allows for the use of your work without permission called the **"Fair Use"** provision. It basically states that someone can use a work for educational or news reporting purposes.

So if you write blog article about a gallery show that was shut down because of raunchy photos, you can add a copy of the photo to your article under the fair use provision. Fair use is intended mainly for non-commercial, non-profit usages. This is where it can get tricky, because if you're simply educating for free, then you're ok, but if your article is used to generate interest in a product you're selling, you may be infringing.

Here are some usages that would be considered Fair Use of your work:

- Educational purposes, like for a teaching lesson
- Research
- News reporting
- Incidental reproduction, in a newsreel or broadcast, of a work located in the scene of an event being reported
- A review or criticism of your art
- A news or biographical article about you and your work
- Using your image to clarify an author's observations in a scholarly or technical work
- A parody of your work
- And more

Section 107 also sets out four factors to be considered in determining whether or not a particular use is fair:

1. The purpose and character of the use, including whether such use is of commercial nature or is for nonprofit educational purposes
2. The nature of the copyrighted work
3. The amount used in relation to the copyrighted work as a whole
4. The effect of the use upon the potential market for, or value of, the copyrighted work

Fair use is a very grey area and not always easy to distinguish from infringement. Ultimately, it's up to the courts to determine.

A lot of people (I see it a lot on YouTube) write something like "I am not the copyright owner, but am posting this work under the fair use clause, this video is copyright John Doe, www.johndoe.com" on their websites or pages. I'm afraid acknowledging the source of the copyrighted material is not a substitute for obtaining permission.

Be Careful When Creating Your Own Work
Most of this ebook is about protecting yourself from having your work stolen, but guess what, these rules apply to you too!

Artists, especially illustrators, digital montage artists and concept artists working on tight deadlines, often use reference from magazine clippings, jpegs off the web, film stills, illustrations, etc., in an effort to speed up their process or achieve a level or realism.

You have to be extremely careful how you use reference for your work. Copying a photo out of a magazine for a character's face is a copyright violation, copying any element actually like the pose, the specific lighting effect, the clothes, the facial expression, a graphic element and much more. Someone took that photo and someone other than you owns the copyright. You can't copy elements of its done in a recognizable way.

Here's on thing I like to do: Instead of finding a pose of a bodybuilder I like and copying that pose for a barbarian painting, I first come up with a pose in my sketchbook, then pull separate body part reference images and combine them to match my sketch. This way my reference is a composite of many anatomical studies and not recognizable as one person's photograph.

There is one exception where you can use photos directly and that is books or websites that are created as reference that **specifically give you permission** to use the photos as you like. An example would be an anatomy book for comic artists which might have photos of nudes in action poses that allows you to copy them if you like. The permissions are often granted in the beginning of a book or the Terms of Use page on a website. Sometimes there are limits on the permission like you can only copy them for non-commercial use.

You can copy an image directly if you ONLY show it as part of your portfolio to showcase your abilities in an effort to secure work. But you can never profit from it. For example, you can do a painting of the *Terminator* and put it in your portfolio to get work, but if you make prints of the painting and sell them, you're infringing on another's rights and could get in big trouble. But ultimately, it's best to be original. An art director is not going to get too excited by a portfolio full of copied photographs of someone else's characters.

If you are a collage artist, things can get complicated. Depending on the context of your commentary with your art, it may fall under the fair use terms, but not likely. Using someone else's work in yours is copyright infringement. I'd do some careful investigation into this issue for your own sake.

If you create an illustration and you relinquish the copyrights, as in the case of a work for hire assignment, even thought you created the image and maybe even the character, if you create a substantially similar work later, repaint the original work, or use the characters or elements of the imagery, you will be infringing on the copyright. You sold your copyrights in that image for the fee of the assignment.

What to do if Your Copyrights are Infringed

You never want to find out that someone has used one of your paintings without permission. Nowadays, infringement is mostly seen on the internet, but it also happens in many other areas, especially commerce. It's a drag, and you are put in an uncomfortable position as to what course of action you should take, if any. Here're some things you can do.

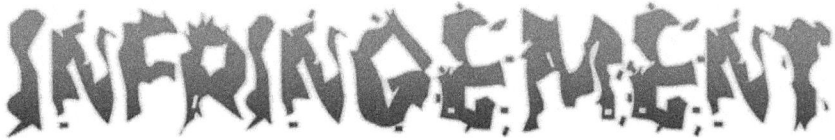

Do Nothing

This may seem strange, but if the infringement is nothing more than a fantasy art fan who made some galleries on his Facebook page for fun because he loves art or printed a few t-shirts for his gaming group, you might consider this to be no big deal (even though it is a copyright infringement) and an opportunity for some free advertising of your work and a wider spread reputation.

In these cases, whether the poster asks permission or I discover the gallery and decide to contact him, I ask that in lieu of payment for the use of my work, he must post the copyright information and a link to my website. This way the posting acts as advertising for my artistic and business pursuits.

Consider that the "Infringement" Might Be a Coincidence

It doesn't happen often, but it is possible that you and another person created a similar image independently, and that there was really no willful infringement. This is very likely if your work is unpublished or has very little distribution.

You can't win a lawsuit if you create a character, register for the copyright, but your drawing sits in a drawer and there is no possible way Steven Spielberg could have seen it to rip it off for his latest movie. Even if it were published, if it is not reasonable that Spielberg would have seen it, you likely won't win a lawsuit.

Consider that the "Infringement" Might be Fair Use
Examine the way your work is used by another. It might actually fall under the fair use provision, in which case you can just let it go. If you still don't like the way it's being used, or if you'd like a link to your site attached to the article, just contact the author or site owner and talk with him.

Open a Dialog
As I said before, the average person does not understand copyrights at all. I'd advise you to be friendly and contact whoever is using your work, whether it's someone who wrote an article and included your artwork or a website owner who is posting your work, and inform him that he is indeed infringing on your rights.

There's nothing wrong with having a friendly conversation with someone about the situation and how to remedy it. If the recipient ignores you or is not interested in complying with your requests, then you may want to move on to other options.
Sometimes it's easy to contact a site owner, like when they've posted their contact info, but sometimes it's not. Every website is required by law to log certain information and that info is available by doing what's called a "whois" search. Many domain registrar sites offer free whois searches where you enter the name of the site and the info comes up. Just Google it.

A whosis search will bring up the domain name registrar, the contact info for the owner of the website, and the internet service provider (ISP). However, anyone can buy whois privacy protection, in which case, an independent company will be listed as the owner and contact person. So then you're out of luck and may need some help to track down the info.

Contact the Website Owner First

When someone illegally posts your copyrighted art, **by law everyone in the chain of distribution is an infringer.** Not only is the person posting liable for willful infringement, but the person or company that owns the website, the site hosting company, and the ISP are all also potentially liable.

In light of this, many websites, especially large ones, have processes in place to help prevent copyright infringement, ways to contact them about it, and they will often intervene on your behalf.

A website company will and ask an infringing user to remove the unauthorized image under threat of losing their account, or simply remove the content automatically.

In the case of a physical infringement, like the use of your art on a physical product like a book that would have to be recalled, a company owner might not be very open to discussion. It might be necessary to work through a lawyer.

Sick the Company on Them

If you see your painting being used illegally and it was a work for hire assignment, contact the company you did the work for. They want to protect their copyright interests just like you do and usually have staff lawyers that will take the appropriate action.

Bring in the Lawyers

You can try to communicate directly with various structures like websites, and ISPs, or you can hire a law firm to set things in motion for you. Lawyers will often get the attention of infringers and companies faster than you can on your own.

Send a "Cease and Desist" Letter

A Cease and Desist Letter is an order for an infringer to halt an activity (cease) and not to take it up again later (desist) or else face legal action. This can be a very effective tactic that tells and infringer that you're not messing around and usually scares him into complying.

A cease and desist letter can be sent to any level of the internet distribution channels. If a site owner or company is not being helpful, you may want to contact their ISP, but doing so on your own might not be easy. In fact, you may not be able to determine a site's ISP without a court order, I'm not sure, but a lawyer could certainly achieve this for you.

Most companies, large and small, comply with a cease and desist letter in order to avoid a copyright infringement lawsuit.

Send a DMCA Take Down Notice
There is an update to the copyright law (Section 512c) called the **Digital Millennium Copyright Act (DMCA),** that has procedures to issue a "take-down notice" to an ISP, where the ISP is required to take down the infringing material when duly notified by the copyright owner in exchange for immunity from infringement responsibility.

The ISP has to registered with the Copyright Office to qualify, and you can search the USCO site by clicking "Online Service Providers" under "Search Copyright Records," then click on "Browse through the OSP directory of designated agents", to find their listing and instructions on how to file a DMCA complaint with them. Many ISPs, large companies, and large website businesses have info on their own site as well.

File a Lawsuit
After you've exhausted all other avenues and having a discussion with your attorney, you may decide that suing the infringing party is your best option. Remember, a lawsuit is very expensive and you have to carefully weight your options. Sometimes it is imperative that you do sue to protect your copyrights and intellectual property assets.

Contract Terms Related to Copyrights

This book is not about the ins and outs of contract terms and negotiations, so I won't be going into too much detail here, but I will hit some of the major points. If you recall, the law stipulates that you can subdivide your copyrights and the following contract stipulations indicate various sub-rights that are being sold in an agreement.

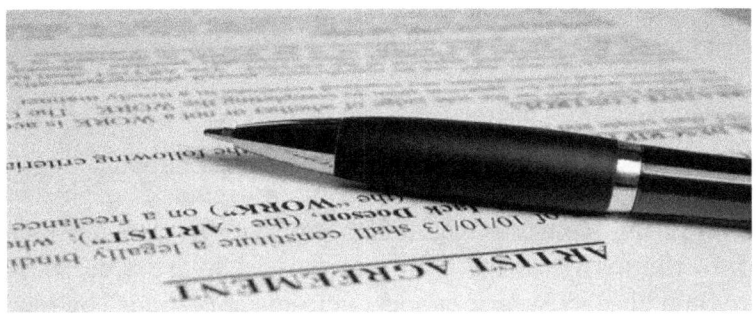

Assignment or Transfer of Rights

Since you instantly, automatically, and exclusively own the copyrights to any piece of art you create, any time you enter an arrangement with someone regarding the use your artwork you are either assigning or transferring all, or some subdivision of, your copyrights to them, which has to be *in writing and signed* by the work's creator.

"Transfer of Rights", **"Assignment of Rights"**, and **"Grant of Rights"** are synonymous terms which mean that you are legally agreeing to give or sell a person or company your copyrights in a work, at which time you no longer own the rights. I some cases, the transfer is temporary if a "term" (or length of time) has been attached; in which case the assignee is allowed to use your copyrights in your work as if they were their own for the agreed upon term. The more rights you assign, the greater your fee and royalties should be.

Definition: An "Assignee" (or "Transferee") is the person or company that you are assigning or transferring your copyrights to. You are the "assignor" or "transferor".

If someone buys an original painting from you, the copyrights DO NOT automatically transfer to them, except the right to display the work publicly. You still own all other copyrights and can exercise them at will. It's good practice to notify the buyers of this fact, because many people that are not in the field don't understand copyrights, so it's your job to educate them.

Termination of Transfers and Reversion of Rights

You should be aware of an often ignored right called **"Termination Rights"**. Rights in a *non work for hire* work **revert back to the artist** (or the family of those who are deceased) after approximately 35 years, under certain conditions by serving written notice on the transferee within specified time limits, even if copyright has been unconditionally sold or licensed to another. So even if you sold the rights by contract, you can reclaim them after 35 years, unless the agreement was a work for hire agreement.

A Copyright is Personal Property

Copyright is a **personal property right**, and it is subject to the state laws and regulations that govern the ownership, inheritance, or transfer of personal property as well as terms of contracts, by which transfers of copyright are normally made. In other words, a copyright is considered an asset by the law, just like a house or stocks, and can be sold, transferred, or willed to your heirs. You should put a stipulation in your will about the transfer of your copyrights to your beneficiaries.

Reproduction and Distribution Rights

Usually the copyrights you are most often transferring in a contract are the reproduction and distribution rights.

Definition: "Reproduction Rights" is the copyright that gives you the creator of a work the exclusive right to make reproductions or copies of the work.

Definition: "Distribution Rights" is the copyright that gives you the creator of a work the exclusive right to distribute those reproductions or copies to the public by sale or other means. It also allows the copyright holder to prevent the unauthorized distribution of copies.

A copyright owner can put **conditions or limits on the rights** that he sells or assigns. He can **subdivide his rights** and sell some and retain some, or sell some to one company, and some to another. He can also **license**, or "rent out", his rights for a fixed period of time, after which time they revert back to him.

It's important that you outline **what rights you are transferring** and **what they can be used for**, the **length of time** they are transferred for, and the **region in which they can be used**, in *every* contract.

An example of contract language might be:

"Artist grants Company the first time publishing rights [grant of rights] *of Work X for use on the "Zombie Rage" book cover and any marketing material used in its promotion* [use limitations], *in the United States only* [region], *wherein the work will not be published by anyone else for a period of three years* [time period]."

Or: *"Artist grants all rights* [grant of rights] *to the images outlined in Appendix A to Licensing Company XYZ in order to produce t-shirts and posters* [use limitations] *with the images featured on it in the country of Japan* [region] *for a period of two years* [time period]."

Common Subdivisions of Reproduction and Display Rights

The following are some of the ways copyrights are commonly subdivided and assigned, and some important issues that should be addressed in any copyright related contract that directly affect the transfer of rights.

All Rights

Just like it sounds, if you sign a contract where you are transferring **all rights**, then you are giving away all your copyrights in a work and can no longer exercise any of them. The assignee now owns the work and the rights to do whatever he wants with them. If you use the work, then you are infringing on their copyright.

Region Restriction of Rights

You should always note the region in which the rights that you are transferring can be exploited. **Worldwide rights** means everywhere on the planet. And something like **North American rights** means the assignee can use your work in North America, but you still retain the right to use the work everywhere else. So if you want to publish a book in Asia, you can, even though you've sold the rights to, and cannot publish in North America.

Term

The **term** is the length of time attached to the assignment of rights. In a sense, you are loaning out your copyrights to a company for a period of time. That period can be any length you want but is commonly something like 2-5 years and contracts often include language spelling out circumstances under which a term to be renewed or extended. If a contract uses the phrase **"in perpetuity"**, that means *forever*.

Reservation of Rights

If you do not specifically spell out rights that you are transferring in a contract, then you still own them by law and they are not transferred. But in the case of the use of a broad term like the transfer of "publishing rights", a lot of rights that you may not have intended or could have predicted might get transferred and you may lose the potential for a lot of future profit.

So it is a good idea to put the following **"reservation of rights" phrase** in any contract: *"All rights not specifically granted herein are reserved to the artist."* This language insures that you retain rights to new technologies that may not have been invented yet, or unforeseen changes in the law.

It's also a good idea to explicitly spell out what rights you *are* transferring, so there is no confusion.

First Time Rights
The best case scenario where copyrights are concerned is for you to grant the company **first time publishing rights**. This means that you own all the copyrights to the image, but you are granting the company you are doing the job for the right to be the first company to publish the work on their product. There is usually a term attached to first time rights so the company has a fair amount of time (often 2 or 3 years) to be the only product in the marketplace with a particular image, after which you are free to sell the image elsewhere if you like.

Secondary Rights
When a work has already been published by one company and the contract term has expired, and you want to sell the rights for the work to be used by another company, you are granting **secondary rights**. Secondary rights commonly sell for a lower fee than all, first time, or exclusive rights. Smaller companies like to buy secondary rights because the get a great painting for a lesser fee; and it's good for you because you get another payment for the same piece you already painted.

Electronic Rights

Electronic rights refers to any digital format that your work can be distributed in including, but not limited to, **ebooks, dvds, cds, digital downloads, streaming, mobile applications, etc.** This is an often difficult, but very important area to retain rights in, especially in this day and age. And example would be if you sell the rights to publish your art book in print to a publisher, but retain the rights to publish the ebook version yourself.

Rights Revert Back

Always include a clause in your contracts that states that if the contract is terminated be either party, the company becomes insolvent (broke or bankrupt), or the project is cancelled before publication, then all rights revert back to you, the creator of the work.

Terms to Look Out For and Avoid in a Contract

When you first get a contract to review, check for these red flag terms. If you see them, you may want to try to negotiate around them. You may choose to sign a contract under some of these terms if you feel it's worth it. I'm just pointing out your best case scenarios. Remember, your work might hit big, and when it does you want to retain as many rights as possible to capitalize on later.

"Work for Hire"
Not at all to your advantage (see below)

"All worldwide rights"
Not horrible, but try to limit the scope to regional or US only territories. Then you can sell the work in foreign markets for a second payday on the same work.

"All rights in perpetuity"
This means they own the rights *forever*. Always try to have the shortest time frame possible on grants of rights. Two to three years is not unreasonable.

"Electronic Rights"
Try to retain as many electronic rights as you can. If a company is adamant about also getting the electronic rights, subdivide them and get very specific about which electronic mediums they can publish in.

"All rights in all formats, now and not invented yet"
This is bad because when a new format like dvds or ebooks, or a new publishing platform technology like iPhones comes out, then the company also owns the rights to publish your work in those formats, and you've lost another opportunity to make future money on your work.

"Non-Compete Clause"
This is often slipped into contracts, especially full time employment contracts, that states that if you leave the company, or finish the contract work, you cannot do similar work for a competing company or similar industry for X amount of time, usually 1-3 years.

Work for Hire Contract
When you sign a **"work for hire" agreement**, you relinquish ALL your copyrights in the works you are contracted to create and assign them to the company you are entering the agreement with. If the contract uses the term "work for hire" *anywhere* in its language, then it IS a work for hire contract.

They own it all, unless the contract grants you back some rights, for a term of 95 years from publication or 120 years from creation, whichever is shorter.

If you are an **employee of a company** when you create a work, that is considered work for hire, and the company owns all the copyrights to anything you create at work, unless some other agreement was struck when you were hired.

Never sign a work for hire contract whenever possible. **In many cases a company does not need to purchase *all* rights in order to accomplish their goals in using your work.** It's your job to understand and stand up for your rights. Do your best to negotiate terms that are more favorable to you than a work for hire contract where you relinquish all your rights.

You're better off changing the phrase "work for hire" to "independent contractor" which means that you are a freelancer and have no official partnership with a company, and that you'll retain any copyrights the explicitly assigned in the agreement. An independent contractor agreement IS NOT a work for hire agreement. Buy read the language carefully, sometimes a contract is called an independent contractor agreement, but it's really a work for hire and is grabbing all the rights.

Another casualty of a work for hire agreement is that you forfeit your Termination Rights and ability to reclaim your copyrights 35 years after publication.

Minimum Rights You Want

If you can't negotiate for a first time publishing rights arrangement, and the company owns all the copyrights to a work, make sure you get the following rights assigned back to you in the contract:

1.) Artist owns the original artwork, paintings and sketches, to do with what he sees fit.

2.) Company grants Artist the following rights, once any images the Artist created for the game are made public:

a.) Display rights for the image and the original painting

b.) Artist may publish the images, as a means of self promotion, in various forms of his portfolio, digital or in print, including but not limited to: online portfolios, websites, blogs, collections of his work, artist showcases, annuals, and other marketing outlets.

c.) Artist is granted the limited rights to produce and sell Artist Prints.

d.) Artist must attach copyright ownership notices to all images in the form of © Year, Company.

3.) If significant changes, other than resizing and color correction, are to be made to the artwork, artist is to do them.

Licensing

Licensing is when you grant permission for your work to be used. A license might be issued for any number of reasons, but **in regards to artwork, the term "licensing" usually means you granting reproduction rights permission for a company to put your imagery on various products or merchandise and offer them for sale.**

Some examples of licensed products are: t-shirts, mugs, stickers, iPhone cases, posters, calendars, greeting cards, action figures, you name it. Think of any item you've ever seen Star Wars on; that's a licensed product.

Licensing is a huge opportunity for you to make money with your artwork and/or intellectual property. But it's not always easy to get a licensing deal, especially if you or your property are not very well known. There are licensing trade shows where you can shop your wares and try to make deals. Licensing is another large topic, so I suggest you look into it when you're ready, but here are some contract items to look for.

Royalties

In exchange for this licensing grant of rights, you receive a fee. In licensing, it's usually a royalty based on merchandise sales ranging anywhere from 5% – 15% on average.

Whenever negotiating a licensing contract, you want to secure an **advance against royalties.** An advance against royalties is when you get a fixed amount of money *up front* that is considered part of your total royalty income. In other words, you don't make any extra royalties until the royalty income adds up to more than the amount of the advance. It's kinda like the company leant you money, and you first pay that advance loan off with your royalty income before you receive royalty payments.

Contract Items

Like other copyright contracts you want to specify terms for all of the things discussed above including: use limitations or specifications, the region, and the term of the licensing deal.

Licensing deals usually spell out conditions for renewing the license. This often takes the form of an automatic renewal if both parties agree in writing, or a renewal predicated on performance, like if royalties equal $10,000 during the 2 year term, the license will renew automatically for another 2 years.

In addition to a renewal based on performance stipulations, some licensing contracts include a "guarantee" clause which states that the licensing company will guarantee the licensor (you) a certain amount of money over the term of the contract. The more famous you or your property are, the more likely you can secure a guarantee, but it doesn't happen often in the beginning.

Licensing deals also specify if you are granting the licensing company **exclusive or non-exclusive us**e of your images. Exclusive use means you are granting use rights to that company *only* and they are the only one that can use image for the term of the contract. A non-exclusive agreement means that the company can use the image to create products, but you can also sell it to other companies to make products. However, you do want to exercise good business sense and not have your licensees competing with each other. You should get paid more for an exclusive deal.

Many companies that license work are also the manufacturer, so it's a good idea to have a clause that allows you to inspect any products and approve the quality of them before they go to production. Manufacturers and publisher often discount merchandise after a period to clear out inventory that isn't selling very well. You may want to have terms in the contract that limit the amount they can discount the merchandise (which would greatly reduce your royalty).

Third Party Assignment or Sublicensing

This is where the contract allows the company that you are assigning the right to, to re-assign them to a third party (someone else). Sometimes this is necessary in the course of business, especially in licensing. You assign Company X the right to use your painting on a variety of merchandise. But they have to be able to assign their sublicense contractor the legal right to actually print the painting image on a t-shirt. So you have to allow third party assignment in your initial contract with Company X. However, you can put stipulations on it or require that you must sign off on it.

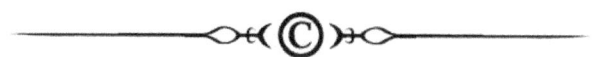

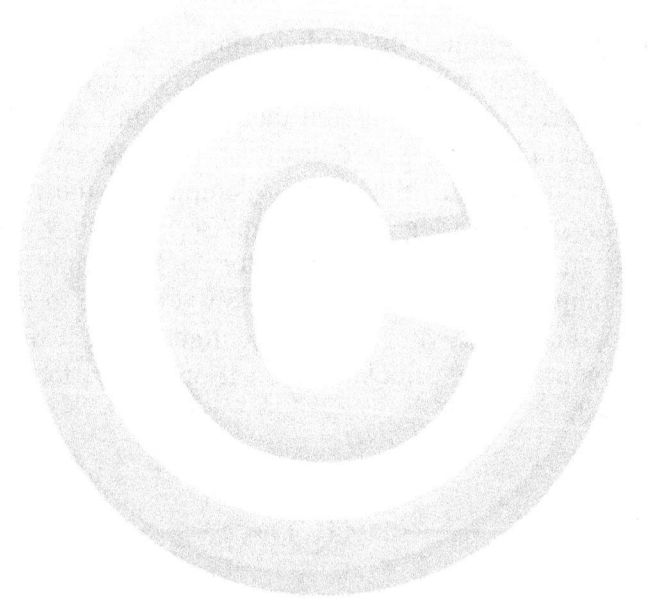

Section 4: Trademark vs Copyright

Copyrights and trademarks are two separate types of protection. It would behoove you to know what copyrights cover and what trademarks cover, so do some research.

Basically a copyright **covers an image** like a *painting* of Superman flying through the air. Trademark **covers the term** "Superman" as pertaining to the character and also **an image that represents a brand** like Superman's "S" chest logo or the Macintosh Apple symbol.

A "mark" is either the word or an image (or a combination of both) that represents a brand. A word mark is often registered as a logo in a specific font, or it can be just the word or phrase (like Wendy's famous "Where's the Beef?" trademarked phrase) that is attached to the brand.

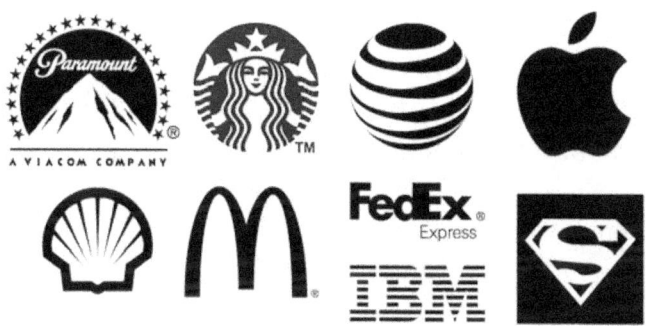

Trademarks have to be applied for and approved and are not automatically protected like a copyrighted creation is.

Trademarks only apply to marks (images or words) that are **actively being used in commerce on goods for sale.** Once there are no goods bearing the trademark being offered for sale, then the mark is dead and ownership is forfeited.

Trademarks are also specific to predetermined goods categories, so I can register a mark called "Dragon Guts" to the t-shirts and apparel category, and someone else can use the same mark in another category like books, so long as I have not registered the mark in that category.

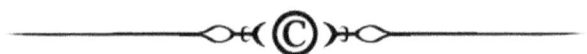

If You Found This Ebook Useful...

I hope you've enjoyed *Copyright Basics for Artists*. I wrote it to help other creatives like myself understand copyrights and how they apply to our work.

You can help other artists by...

Writing a review on Amazon
Sharing news about this book on social media
Telling your artist friends how helpful it was

Thanks, Tom

About Tom Baxa

I've been a professional fantasy illustrator for over 25 years! My career has been filled with a wide variety of high end clients in the rpg, ccg, miniatures, video games, and film industries such as Dungeons and Dragons, Shadowrun, Vampire, Magic the Gathering, and World of Warcraft.

My work has appeared on the covers and interiors of countless books and magazines (including *Spectrum*), and my concept designs have contributed to many cool video game and movie projects.

As I continue to freelance as an illustrator and concept artist in Los Angeles, my main focus is on developing my own projects, both as an artist and an author, and growing the BaxaArt brand including its newest addition BaxaArtAcademy.com, whose mission is to provide a virtual mentorship for artists of all levels through demos, tutorials, information, and professional experience as a springboard to a fulfilling career as a fantasy artist and personal artistic growth.

Check out my website www.BaxaArt.com for great art, merchandise, prints, and paintings for sale, as well as my art book *Blood Rituals: The Art of Tom Baxa*. My blog is full of updates about my work, helpful information, stories about my life as an artist, cool art by me and my friends and much more: *BaxaArt Blog*, http://baxaart.blogspot.com.

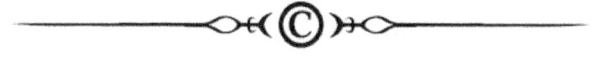

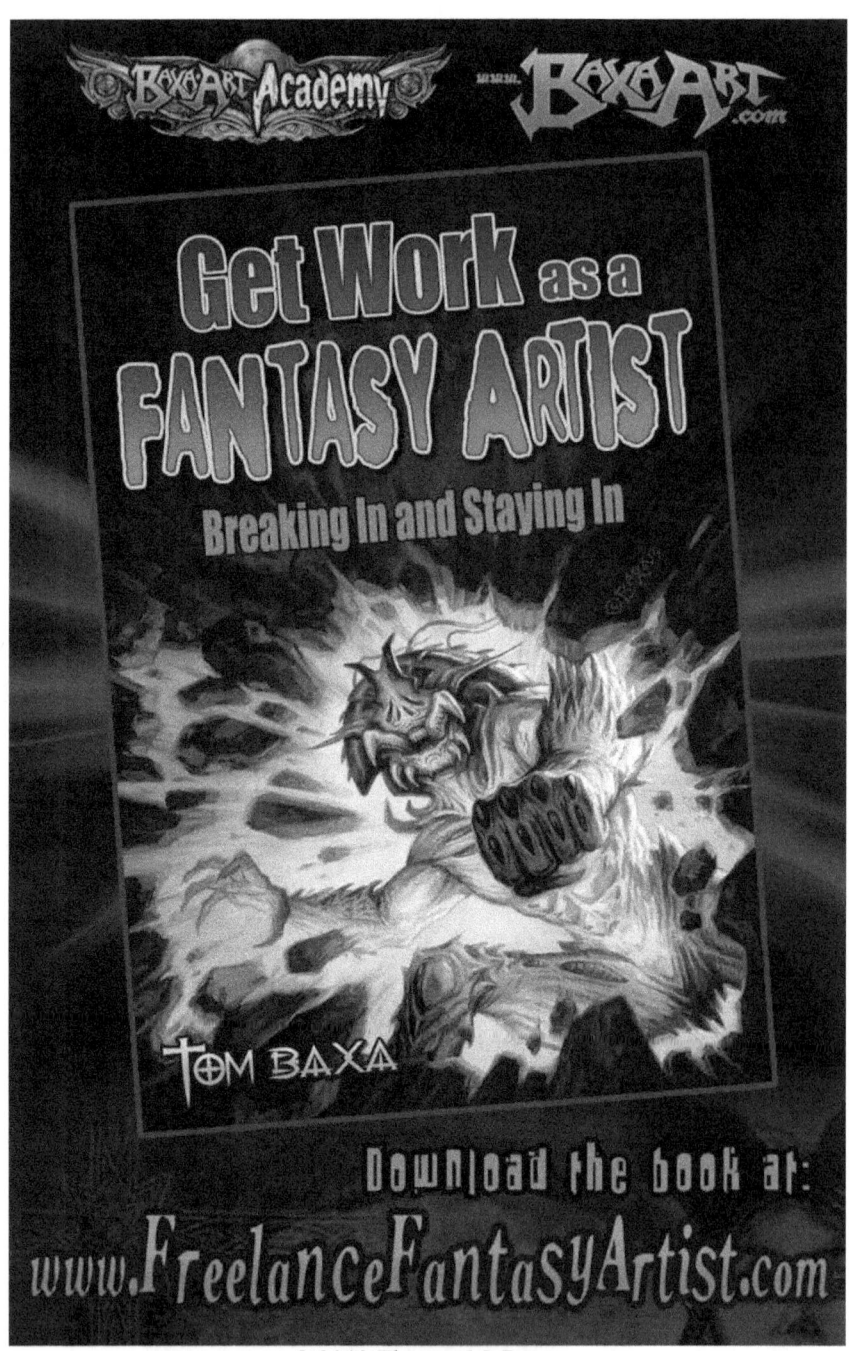

Insider Secrets - www.FreelanceFantasyArtist.com

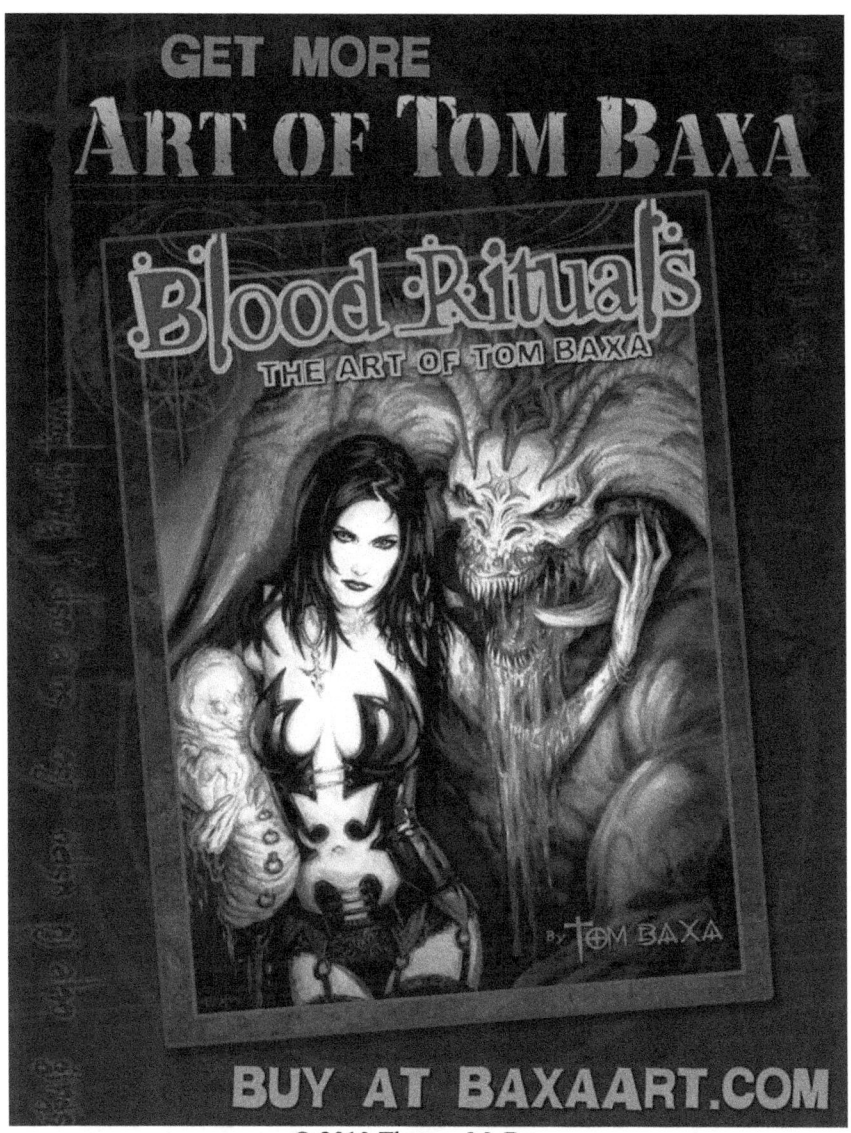
APPENDIX

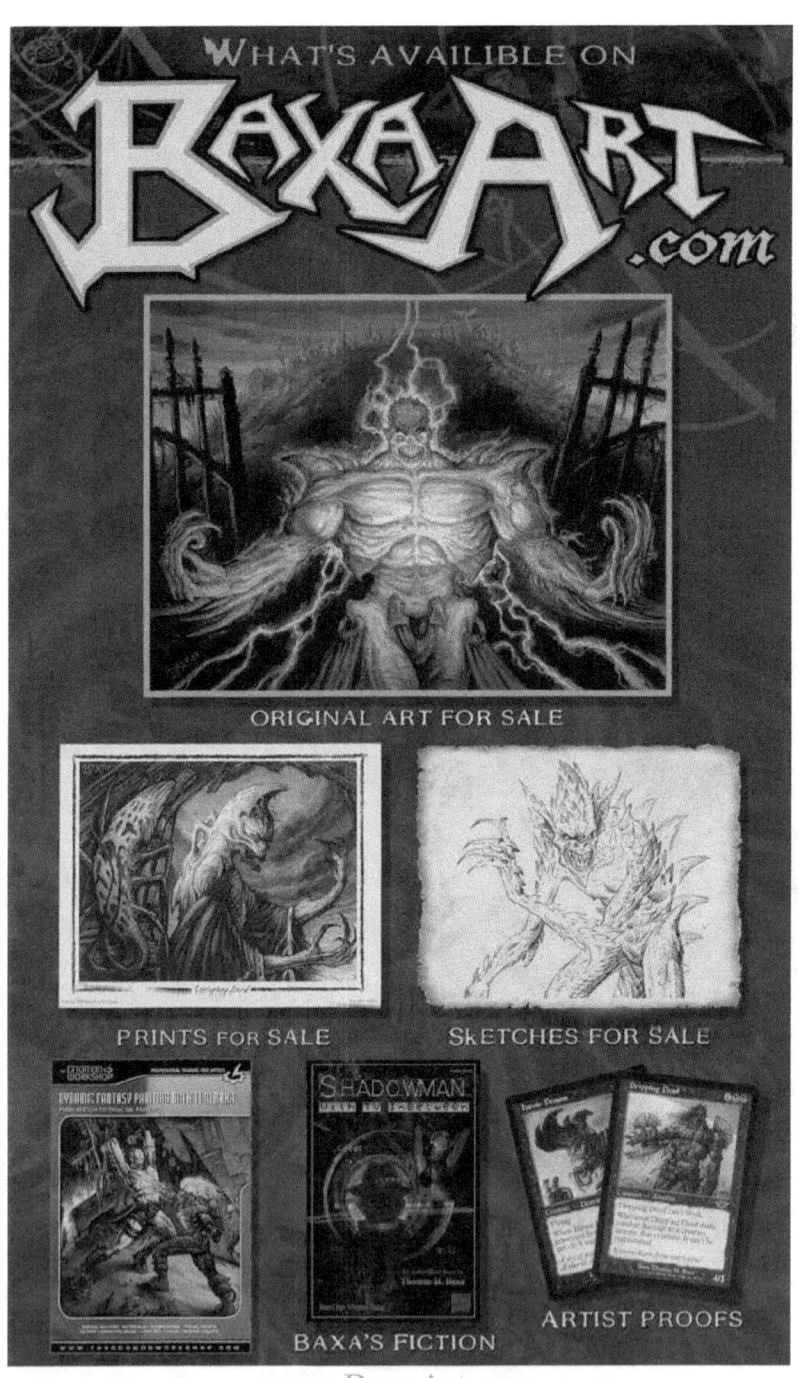

APPENDIX

www.ingramcontent.com/pod-product-compliance
Lightning Source LLC
Chambersburg PA
CBHW072247170526
45158CB00003BA/1025